$\mathcal{P}$OPE $\mathcal{B}$ENEDICT XVI

POPE BENEDICT XVI

IN MY OWN WORDS

Compiled and Edited by
Daniel J. Michaels, PhD

Liguori
LIGUORI, MISSOURI

Imprimi Potest:
Thomas D. Picton, C.Ss.R.
Provincial, Denver Province
The Redemptorists

Published by Liguori Publications
Liguori, Missouri
www.liguori.org

Introduction and compilation © 2005 by Daniel T. Michaels
Words of Pope Benedict XVI © 2005
by Libreria Editice Vaticana

Interior photographs: Catholic News Service © 2005

Library of Congress Cataloging-in-Publication Data

Benedict XVI, Pope, 1927–
    In my own words / Pope Benedict XVI ; compiled and edited by Daniel T. Michaels.
        p. cm.
    ISBN 0-7648-1382-X (hardcover)
    1. Catholic Church—Doctrines. I. Michaels, Daniel T. II. Title.
BX1751.3.B46 2005
230'.2—dc22   2005025965

Liguori Publications, a nonprofit corporation, is an apostolate of the Redemptorists. To learn more about the Redemptorists, visit *Redemptorists.com.*

Printed in the United States of America
09 08 07 06 05 5 4 3 2 1
First edition

CONTENTS

$\mathcal{I}$NTRODUCTION

Few people today are asked (literally) to *lay
down their lives for Jesus* (see John 13:38). Fewer
actually do so. In April of 1945, a young Joseph
Ratzinger bravely rejected his military duty to
return, body and soul, to the institution that
had formed him from the beginning. Passing
through armed patrols, the young soldier of
Christ miraculously escaped execution and
found his way back to his family, back to his
Church, and back to his religious vocation,
which would one day flower into the highest
ecclesial office.

In retrospect, one can see how this radical
defection not only delimited the major events
of his life—from Catholic youth to soldier;
then from theologian to prelate—but it also
provided an abstract indicator of the religious,
political, and theological issues that made up his
system of belief and understanding of Church
government. In other words, faced with death,
the man who would become Pope Benedict
XVI began a lifelong devotion to the ultimate

questions of life: What is truth? What is love, and how do we express it? Despite praise by some and criticism from others, the pope appears to continually renew his vow of defection from secular power in favor of the institution that teaches us to *lay down our lives for Jesus*. "Do not be afraid," he says, echoing his predecessor, "do not be afraid!"

Childhood

Joseph Ratzinger, the youngest of three children, was born in Marktl am Inn, Germany (rural Bavaria), to Joseph and Maria Ratzinger on April 16, 1927—Holy Saturday—and was baptized immediately in the waters of the Easter Vigil. According to Bavarian custom, his timely birth was considered providential, as it symbolized the nature of human life: "We still await Easter," recalled the pope when asked about his birth. "We do not stand in the fullness of light, but walk toward it full of trust."

Benedict XVI was raised in a Catholic cradle. Although born into a world of great political chaos, with the Weimar Republic in decline and the Nazis rising to power, his early years were filled with happy memories of family and devotion. He recalls again and again how his mother brought him to various pilgrimage sites where he developed a fondness for the mother of God; how he was inspired by the simplicity and humility of the saints; and how his father, a policeman, rejected the new political order and spent much of his time silently protecting the Catholic community.

As a young child his family lived in an ancient *Stift*, a home that in previous centuries was occupied by communities of secular priests. Surrounded by cracked floors, ancient staircases, vaulted ceilings, and crooked rooms, Joseph was steeped in the aura of Baroque monasticism. Once home to the Augustinian canons, his village was lovingly looked after by English Sisters and devoted diocesan pastors.

Due to his father's opposition to the Nazi party, in 1932 the family moved to the village of Aschau, where Joseph began his formal education in primary school. On January 30, 1933, Hindenburg transferred power to Hitler as chancellor of the Reich, and young Joseph, then only age six, was forced to join the so-called "brown shirts" (Nazis) as a member of the Hitler Youth. Admittedly, he formed his first impression of the party through the negative assessments of his father, but shortly after the Nazi ascent to power, Joseph realized firsthand its devastating impact on Catholicism. Christianity was criticized as the destroyer of cultural identity and, therefore, the educational system was reformed in order to gradually eliminate pastoral and theological learning. This oppressive structure heightened Joseph's awareness of the importance of the Church in his community: "[Bavarians] enjoyed a firm symbiosis with the faith of the Church: birth and death, weddings and illnesses, sowing time and harvest time—everything was encompassed by the faith." The Reich may have altered the people's lifestyle, but it could not change their hearts.

As political tension increased, the Catholic community of Aschau rallied around the liturgy. Outside of the *Gymnasium* (the German equivalent to college prep school) the liturgy was the only way to nurture Catholic education in their village. While Joseph was still learning to read, his parents introduced him to the *Schott*, a revolutionary translation of the Roman Missal into German. "Every new step into the liturgy was a great event for me," recalled the pope from those early years: "It was a riveting adventure to move by degrees into the mysterious world of the liturgy." His childhood love for the liturgy would later impact his influence and response to the Second Vatican Council.

On March 6, 1937, Joseph's father turned sixty, the mandatory age for retirement, and the family was moved to Traunstein. Joseph entered the *Gymnasium* to study classical languages (Greek and Latin). As the youngest and smallest student in his school, he was armed only with a gentle shyness and introverted curiosity. He excelled in his studies, and after two years the pastor recommended that Joseph—then only twelve years old—enter the minor seminary.

By 1940 no one could ignore the massive movement of troops. The war spread to France, Czechoslovakia, and Poland, and the minor seminary was declared a military hospital. Hitler quickly conquered Denmark, Norway, Holland, Belgium, Luxembourg, and the Balkins. As Ratzinger noted in his memoir, "Even [Germans] who were completely opposed to National Socialism [Nazism] experienced some level of patriotic satisfaction." By 1941, however, Germany attacked the Soviet Union, extending the front line from the North Pole to the Black Sea, and German casualties made their way to Traunstein. Huge transports of wounded filled the makeshift hospitals once home to schools and seminaries. In 1943, at age sixteen, while still studying in the seminary, Joseph was drafted to serve the batteries of the antiaircraft defense (known as the *Flak*). His class was moved to Ludwigsfeld, north of Munich, where they divided time between books and guns.

Despite the bleak historical circumstances, young Joseph was beginning to find new expression to his childhood faith through his education. He immersed himself in the Greek and Latin classics, mathematics, and, above all, literature. He also began to write with great zeal, returning with joy to the liturgical texts (*Schott*) of his youth. Armed with the classics, he attempted to translate the liturgy in an improved and more vital way. "This was a time of interior exultation," he remembers, "full of hope for the great things that were gradually opening up to me in the boundless realm of the spirit."

On September 10, 1944, Joseph reached military age and was drafted into a regular army labor unit, building blockades and digging trenches as the line moved progressively deeper into Germany. By the end of April 1945, however, he realized that the liturgy of war was completely void of meaning; it was time to become a soldier of Christ, and a supporter of the true liturgy of God. Risking execution, he defected to his home where he was reunited with his family. Hitler died, and eventually the Americans made their way to Traunstein. Joseph was identified as an active soldier and detained for evaluation. After serving a brief sentence in a prisoner-of-war camp, he was reintroduced into priestly formation, where, for the first time since his childhood, he had the freedom to participate in and help form a vibrant Catholic ethos in his homeland.

Priesthood and Academic Life

Following the war, Joseph studied philosophy in the seminary at Freising and theology at the University of Munich. Like a child with newfound freedom, he applied his classical training and real-life (and loss of life) experience to the works of the greatest Roman Catholic minds of the twentieth century. Romano Guardini, Michael Schmaus, Joseph Pieper, Odo Casel, and Henri de Lubac, in particular, had a lasting effect on his personal theological vision. Ratzinger was quickly identified as one of the most intelligent members of his class. He was ordained to the priesthood in Freising during the summer of 1951. Two years later he received his doctorate of theology—writing on Saint Augustine's ecclesiology—and was assigned to lecture alongside the all-star theologians of his former seminary at Freising.

After graduation, he began studying the theology of the great medieval theologian Saint Bonaventure (+1274), an endeavor that would shape his understanding of history and salvation. This research qualified him for a second doctorate two years later, enabling him to serve as lecturer at the University of Munich and as professor of fundamental theology and dogma at the College of Philosophy and Theology at Freising.

In 1959, at the young age of thirty-two, he became the ordinary professor of fundamental theology at the University of Bonn. During this time he worked alongside Cardinal Frings of Cologne, who was a member of the Central Preparatory Commission for the Second Vatican Council. As the cardinal's theological advisor, Ratzinger was sent to Rome where he was named a *peritus* ("expert") of the Council. By the time the Council issued its first decree in 1963, he had accepted the chair of dogmatic theology at the University of Münster, and thus shared service between Rome and Germany.

By the summer of 1966, he joined the Catholic faculty at the ecumenical university in Tübingen, the theological hot-spot of Germany at the time. Although this theological climate stimulated some of his most important work, these years solidified his rejection of overzealous idealism. In 1968 there was a Marxist revolution that, according to Ratzinger, led to the destruction of theology. "It took biblical hope as its basis but inverted it by keeping the religious ardor but eliminating God and replacing him with the political activity of man. Hope remains, but the party takes the place of God, and, along with the party, a totalitarianism that practices an atheistic sort of adoration ready to sacrifice all humanness to its false god." Therefore, fearing the ideological tendencies that ruled his childhood, Ratzinger began to champion a more traditional theological approach.

In 1969 he welcomed the invitation to form a theological faculty at the recently opened university of Regensburg, where he joined a team of scholars to complete a massive nine-volume study of Christian doctrine. His most significant contribution to this project was a volume on eschatology, death, and eternal life—topics that reflect the most important themes of his youth.

In the years that followed, Joseph Ratzinger would publish more than thirty volumes of theology, placing him among the most influential theologians of the twentieth century. His works covered a wide range of topics: ecclesiology, salvation history, revelation, liturgy, preaching, catechesis, and eschatology. As his theological vision unfolded, he clarified with greater emphasis the significance of objective truth. The catastrophic events of his youth provide the basis for his understanding of Christian unity, the Church in the World, and dialogue with other religions. The fundamental insight of his long-ago defection from military service is his insistence that religious truth cannot and should not be suppressed: Catholic Tradition is a gift worth preserving.

In 1977, Joseph Ratzinger was ordained archbishop of Munich-Freising, and shortly afterward Pope Paul VI named him cardinal. Not surprisingly, he chose as his motto "Fellow Worker in the Truth" (see 3 John 1:8), a phrase which has followed him all the way to the papacy. As Benedict XVI explains, this text summarizes the two poles of his thinking: "For one, the motto seems to provide the connection between my previous task as teacher and my new mission and also because in today's world the theme of truth has all but disappeared." In 1981 he was appointed prefect of the Congregation for the Doctrine of the Faith (CDF), the office charged with defending orthodoxy in virtually every area of Church life.

To much of the world, Ratzinger has been known as the Church's enforcer, "the last check on everything, the final word on orthodoxy." As leader of the CDF, he was charged with the task of excommunicating theologians, approving certain books, rewriting liturgical texts, setting boundaries on ecumenical dialogue, directing Church bureaucracy, and handling Church scandals throughout the world.

Pope Benedict XVI

With his election as pope, Benedict begins a third phase of his life. Long ago he left behind his spade and rifle in favor of religious freedom. In the years that followed, he forged an academic legacy and theological guard as a priest and leader in the Church. Now, as pope, he shares the fullness of his experience with Catholic faithful throughout the world. Since his elevation it has become apparent that he has not forgotten the Catholic compassion that characterized his formation. Now that he has moved from head of the CDF to supreme pontiff—that is from hall monitor to principal—we can observe how his understanding of Tradition and his zeal for truth provide hope for the future of the Church. Throughout the decades his influence has been felt through the words of his theology and his enforcement of doctrine. Now he is known by his actions rather than his reactions.

The following pages provide a portal into the emerging pontificate of Pope Benedict XVI. Quotes from the pope's "own words"—taken from his speeches, homilies, letters, and prayers—give the faithful a snapshot of the pastoral and theological challenges of his first four months in office: Truth and Freedom, Church and Culture, Christian Unity, Eucharist, Ministry, Family and Youth, and Mary. This introductory collection of his words confirms his trust in the Lord, and his conviction that the Church will go forward.

$\mathcal{P}$OPE $\mathcal{B}$ENEDICT XVI

$\mathcal{T}$RUTH:
FREEDOM IN THE
WORD OF GOD

Tossed by the Waves and Swept by the Wind

We should speak of the "measure of the fullness of Christ," which we are called to reach in order to be true adults in the faith. We should not remain infants in faith, in a state of minority. And what does it mean to be an infant in faith? Saint Paul answers: It means "tossed by waves and swept along by every wind of teaching arising from human trickery" (Ephesians 4:14). This description is very relevant today!

How many winds of doctrine we have known in recent decades, how many ideological currents, how many ways of thinking. The small boat of thought of many Christians has often been tossed about by these waves—thrown from one extreme to the other. Every day new sects are created and what Saint Paul says about human trickery comes true, with cunning that tries to draw those into error (see Ephesians 4:14). Having a clear faith based on the creed of the Church is often labeled today as fundamentalism. Whereas relativism, which is letting oneself be tossed and "swept along by every wind of teaching," looks like the only attitude up to today's standards. We are moving toward a dictatorship of relativism that does not recognize anything as certain and has as its highest goal one's own ego and one's own desires.

However, we have a different goal: the Son of God, true man. He is the measure of true humanism. Being an "adult" means having a faith that does not follow the waves of fashion or the latest novelties; an adult and mature faith is deeply rooted in friendship with Christ. It is this friendship that opens us up to all that is good and gives us the knowledge to judge the true from the false and deceit from truth. We must become mature in this adult faith; we must lead the flock of Christ to this faith. And it is this faith—faith alone—that creates unity and is realized. On this theme Saint Paul offers us some beautiful words—in contrast to the continual ups and downs of those who, like infants, are tossed about by the waves: Make truth in love, as the basic formula of Christian existence. In Christ, truth and love coincide. To the extent that we draw near to Christ in our own life, truth and love merge. Love without truth would be blind; truth without love would be like "a resounding gong or a clashing cymbal" (1 Corinthians 13:1).

CARDINAL JOSEPH RATZINGER, HOMILY FOR THE
OPENING OF THE CONCLAVE

Friends With Jesus

At the hour in the Garden of Gethsemane Jesus transformed our rebellious human will into a will shaped and united to the divine will. He suffered the whole experience of our autonomy—and precisely by delivering our will into the hands of God he gave us true freedom: "Not my will, but your will be done." In this communion of wills our redemption takes place: Being friends of Jesus, we become friends of God. How much more we love Jesus, how much better do we know him, how much more does our true freedom grow as well as our joy in being redeemed. Thank you, Jesus, for your friendship!

CARDINAL JOSEPH RATZINGER, HOMILY FOR THE
OPENING OF THE CONCLAVE

Guided by the Spirit of Truth

Without the Holy Spirit, the Church would be reduced to merely a human organization, weighed down by its own structures. But, for its part, in the plans of God, the Spirit habitually makes use of human mediations to act in history. Precisely for this,

Christ, who established the Church on the foundation of the Apostles closely around Peter, has also given it the gift of his Spirit, so that throughout the centuries he would be the comfort (see John 14:16) and the guide to the entire truth (see John 16:13).

REGINA CAELI, MAY 15, 2005

Catholic Faith in the New Millennium

Dear brothers and sisters, how necessary it is at the beginning of this third millennium that the entire Christian community, unanimously and of one accord, proclaim, teach, and witness to the full to the truths of the Catholic faith, doctrine, and morals!

ANGELUS, JULY 3, 2005

No Other Revelation but Christ

In Jesus, God gave us his whole self, that is, he gave us everything. As well as or together with this, there can be no other revelation which can communicate more or in some way complete the Revelation of Christ. In him, in the Son, all has been said to us, all has been given.

HOMILY AT THE BASILICA OF
ST. JOHN LATERAN, MAY 7, 2005

The Voice of the Living Church

Science alone cannot provide us with a definitive and binding interpretation; it is unable to offer us, in its interpretation, that certainty with which we can live and for which we can even die. A greater mandate is necessary for this, which cannot derive from human abilities alone. The voice of the living Church is essential for this, of the Church entrusted until the end of time to Peter and to the College of the Apostles.

This power of teaching frightens many people in and outside the Church. They wonder whether freedom of conscience is threatened or whether it is a presumption opposed to freedom of thought. It is not like this. The power that Christ conferred upon Peter and his Successors is, in an absolute sense, a mandate to serve. The power of teaching in the Church involves a commitment to the service of obedience to the faith. The pope is not an absolute monarch whose thoughts and desires are law. On the contrary: the pope's ministry is a guarantee of obedience to Christ and to his Word. He must not proclaim his own ideas, but rather constantly bind himself and the Church to obedience to God's Word, in the face of every attempt to adapt it or water it down, and every form of opportunism.

Homily at the Basilica of
St. John Lateran, May 7, 2005

Serving the Word of God

The pope knows that in his important decisions, he is bound to the great community of faith of all times, to the binding interpretations that have developed throughout the Church's pilgrimage. Thus, his power is not being above, but at the service of, the Word of God. It is incumbent upon him to ensure that this Word continues to be present in its greatness and to resound in its purity, so that it is not torn to pieces by continuous changes in usage.

The Chair is—let us say it again—a symbol of the power of teaching, which is a power of obedience and service, so that the Word of God—the truth!—may shine out among us and show us the way of life.

Homily at the Basilica of
St. John Lateran, May 7, 2005

The Dawn of the New Heavens and New Earth

History, in fact, is not in the hands of the powers of darkness, chance or human decisions alone. When evil energy that we see is unleashed, when Satan vehemently bursts in, when a multitude of scourges and ills surface, the Lord, the supreme arbiter of historical events, arises. He leads history wisely towards the dawn of the new heavens and the new earth of which, in the image of the New Jerusalem, the last part of the Book of Revelation sings (see Revelation 21—22)....

There is consequently a desire to reaffirm that God is not indifferent to human events but penetrates them, creating his own "ways" or, in other words, his effective plans and "deeds."

GENERAL AUDIENCE, MAY 11, 2005

The Compass of the Spirit

Naturally, I am aware and we all know that many are not immediately able to identify themselves with, to understand, to assimilate all that the Church teaches. It seems to me important firstly to awaken this intention to believe with the Church, even if personally someone may not yet have assimilated many particulars. It is necessary to have this will to believe with the Church, to have trust that this Church—the community not only of two thousand years of pilgrimage of the people of God, but the community that embraces heaven and earth, the community where all the righteous of all times are therefore present—that this Church enlivened by the Holy Spirit truly carries within the "compass" of the Spirit and therefore is the true subject of faith.

ADDRESS TO THE CLERGY OF ROME, MAY 13, 2005

Christ Frees Us From Fear

The words of Pope John Paul II constantly echo in my ears: "Do not be afraid! Open wide the doors for Christ!" The pope was addressing the mighty, the powerful of this world, who feared that Christ might take away something of their power if they were to let him in, if they were to allow the faith to be free. Yes, he would certainly have taken something away from them: the dominion of corruption, the manipulation of law and the freedom to do as they pleased. But he would not have taken away anything that pertains to human freedom or dignity, or to the building of a just society. The Pope was also speaking to everyone, especially the young. Are we not perhaps all afraid in some way? If we let Christ enter fully into our lives, if we open ourselves totally to him, are we not afraid that he might take something away from us? Are we not perhaps afraid to give up something significant, something unique, something that makes life so beautiful? Do we not then risk ending up diminished and deprived of our freedom? And once again the pope said: No! If we let Christ into our lives, we lose nothing, nothing, absolutely nothing of what makes life free, beautiful and great. No! Only in this friendship are the doors of life opened wide. Only in this friendship is the great potential of human existence truly revealed. Only in this friendship do we experience beauty and liberation. And so, today, with great strength and great conviction, on the basis of long personal experience of life, I say to you, dear young people: Do not be afraid of Christ! He takes nothing away, and he gives you everything. When we give ourselves to him, we receive a hundredfold in return. Yes, open, open wide the doors to Christ—and you will find true life. Amen.

HOMILY AT THE IMPOSITION OF THE PALLIUM AND CONFERRAL OF THE FISHERMAN'S RING, APRIL 24, 2005

The Challenge of Relativism

A particularly insidious obstacle to the task of educating is the massive presence in our society and culture of that relativism which, recognizing nothing as definitive, leaves as the ultimate criterion only the self with its desires. And under the semblance of freedom it becomes a prison for each one, for it separates people from one another, locking each person into his or her own "ego."

With such a relativistic horizon, therefore, real education is not possible without the light of the truth; sooner or later, every person is in fact condemned to doubting in the goodness of his or her own life and the relationships of which it consists, the validity of his or her commitment to build with others something in common.

Consequently, it is clear that not only must we seek to get the better of relativism in our work of forming people, but we are also called to counter its destructive predominance in society and culture.

ADDRESS TO THE ECCLESIAL DIOCESAN CONVENTION OF ROME, JUNE 6, 2005

God's Gift of Humanity

The desire to uphold the common good is founded on the belief that man comes into the world as a gift of the Creator. It is from God that all men and women—made in his image— receive their common inviolable dignity and their summons to responsibility. Today, when individuals often forget their origin and thus lose sight of their goal, they easily fall prey to whimsical social trends, the distortion of reason by particular interest groups, and exaggerated individualism. Confronted with this "crisis of meaning" (Encyclical Letter *Fides et Ratio*, 81), civic and religious authorities are called to work together encouraging everyone, including the young, to "direct their steps towards a truth which transcends them" (*ibid.*, 5). Sundered from that universal truth, which is the only guarantee of freedom and happiness, individuals are at the mercy of caprice and slowly lose the capacity to discover the profoundly satisfying meaning of human life.

ADDRESS TO THE AMBASSADOR
OF NEW ZEALAND, JUNE 16, 2005

Secularization

The disquieting process of secularization is occurring in many parts of the world. Where the Christian foundations of society risk being forgotten, the task of preserving the transcendent dimension present in every culture and of strengthening the authentic exercise of individual freedom against relativism becomes increasingly difficult. Such a predicament calls for both Church and civil leaders to ensure that the question of morality is given ample discussion in the public forum. In this regard, there is a great need today to recover a vision of the mutual relationship between civil law and moral law which, as well as being proposed by the Christian tradition, is also part of the patrimony of the great juridical traditions of humanity (see the Enyclical Letter, *Evangelium Vitae*, 71). Only in this way can the multiple claims to "rights" be linked to truth and the nature of authentic freedom be correctly understood in relation to that truth which sets its limits and reveals its goals.

ADDRESS TO THE AMBASSADOR
OF NEW ZEALAND, JUNE 16, 2005

The Revolution of the Saints

The saints…are the true reformers. Now I want to express this in an even more radical way: only from the saints, only from God, does true revolution come, the definitive way to change the world. In the last century we experienced revolutions with a common program—expecting nothing more from God, they assumed total responsibility for the cause of the world in order to change it. And this, as we saw, meant that a human and partial point of view was always taken as an absolute guiding principle. Absolutizing what is not absolute but relative is called totalitarianism. It does not liberate man, but takes away his dignity and enslaves him. It is not ideologies that save the world, but only a return to the living God, our Creator, the guarantor of our freedom, the guarantor of what is really good and true. True revolution consists in simply turning to God who is the measure of what is right and who at the same time is everlasting love. And what could ever save us apart from love?

YOUTH VIGIL, WORLD YOUTH DAY, COLOGNE, GERMANY, AUGUST 20, 2005

The True Face of God

There are many who speak of God; some even preach hatred and perpetrate violence in God's name. So it is important to discover the true face of God. The Magi from the East found it, when they knelt down before the child of Bethlehem. "Anyone who has seen me has seen the Father," said Jesus to Philip (John 14:9). In Jesus Christ, who allowed his heart to be pierced for us, the true face of God is seen. We will follow him together with the great multitude of those who went before us. Then we will be traveling along the right path.

This means that we are not constructing a private God, a private Jesus, but that we

believe and worship the Jesus who is manifested
to us by the sacred Scriptures and who reveals
himself to be alive in the great procession of
the faithful called the Church, always alongside
us and always before us.

YOUTH VIGIL, WORLD YOUTH DAY,
COLOGNE, GERMANY, AUGUST 20, 2005

Faith and Reason

Indeed, knowledge enlightened by faith,
far from dividing communities, binds peoples
together in the common search for truth which
defines every human as one who lives by belief
(see *Fides et Ratio*, 31).

ADDRESS TO THE AMBASSADOR OF THE FORMER
YUGOSLAV REPUBLIC OF MACEDONIA
TO THE HOLY SEE, MAY 19, 2005

Adoration

The Greek word [for adoration,
proskynesis] ...refers to the gesture of sub-
mission, the recognition of God as our true
measure, supplying the norm that we choose to
follow. It means that freedom is not simply
about enjoying life in total autonomy, but

rather about living by the measure of truth and goodness, so that we ourselves can become true and good. This gesture is necessary even if initially our yearning for freedom makes us inclined to resist it.

Homily at World Youth Day, August 21, 2005

Dialogue Toward Truth

It is the Lord's command, but also the imperative of the present hour, to carry on dialogue, with conviction, at all levels of the Church's life. This must obviously take place with sincerity and realism, with patience and perseverance, in complete fidelity to the dictates of one's conscience. There can be no dialogue at the expense of truth; the dialogue must advance in charity and in truth.

Ecumenical Meeting, August 21, 2005

Truth, Justice, and Solidarity

In order to respond effectively to the people's aspirations for true peace, a gift that comes to us from God, it is also our duty to commit ourselves to building it on the firm foundations of truth, justice, and solidarity.

ADDRESS TO THE AMBASSADOR OF THE REPUBLIC OF GUINEA, JUNE 16, 2005

The Good, True, and Beautiful

Just as Cyril and Methodius recognized the acute need to transpose correctly biblical notions and Greek theological concepts into a very different context of thought and historical experience, so today the primary task facing Christians in Europe is that of casting the ennobling light of Revelation on all that is good, true, and beautiful. In this way all peoples and nations are drawn towards that peace and freedom which God the Creator intends for everyone.

ADDRESS TO THE AMBASSADOR OF THE FORMER YUGOSLAV REPUBLIC OF MACEDONIA, MAY 19, 2005

Civil Rights of Religious Freedom

The Church's diplomatic relations form a part of her mission of service to the international community. Her engagement with civil society is anchored in the conviction that the task of building a more just world must acknowledge and consider man's supernatural vocation. The Holy See strives therefore to promote an understanding of the human person who "receives from God his essential dignity and with it the capacity to transcend every social order so as to move towards truth and goodness" (Encyclical Letter *Centesimus Annus*, 38). From this foundation the Church applies the universal values which safeguard the dignity of every person and serve the common good to the vast array of cultures and nations that constitute our world....

It is to faith communities that political and civic authorities can turn for a determined commitment to shaping the social order in accordance with the common good. Such commitment demands that religious freedom, which preserves the singularity of each faith community, be sanctioned as a fundamental civil right and afforded protection by a robust framework of juridical norms which respect the laws and duties proper to religious communities (Vatican II, *Dignitatis Humanae*, 2). Such practical support of religious freedom by political leaders becomes a sure means for authentic social progress and peace.

ADDRESS TO THE AMBASSADOR OF THE
REPUBLIC OF AZERBAIJAN, JUNE 16, 2005

Finding the Face of God

The [Western] world is weary of its own culture. It is a world that has reached the time when there is no longer any evidence of the need for God, let alone Christ, and when it therefore seems that humans could build themselves on their own. In this atmosphere of a rationalism closing in on itself and that regards the model of the sciences as the only model of knowledge, everything else is subjective. Christian life too, of course, becomes a choice that is subjective, hence, arbitrary and no longer the path of life. It therefore naturally becomes difficult to believe, and if it is difficult to believe it is even more difficult to offer one's life to the Lord to be his servant.

...[T]he first answer is patience, in the certainty that the world cannot live without God, the God of Revelation—and not just any God: we see how dangerous a cruel God, an untrue God can be—the God who showed us his Face in Jesus Christ. This Face of the One who suffered for us, this loving Face of the One who transforms the world in the manner of the grain of wheat that fell into the earth....

We ourselves must have a renewed certainty: he is the Truth; only by walking in his footsteps do we go in the right direction, and it is in this direction that we must walk and lead others....

In the end, faith is simple and rich: we believe that God exists, that God counts; but which God? A God with a face, a human face, a God who reconciles, who overcomes hatred and gives us the power of peace that no one else can give us. We must make people understand that Christianity is actually very simple and consequently very rich.

ADDRESS TO DIOCESAN CLERGY
OF AOSTA, JULY 25, 2005

Solidified Humanity

We have before us a common obligation:
We are called together to build a more free,
more peaceful and more solidified humanity.

ADDRESS TO THE PRESIDENT
OF BULGARIA, MAY 23, 2005

CULTURE:
THE CHURCH
IN DIALOGUE
WITH THE WORLD

Peace in Society

I come from a country where peace and brotherhood are treasured by all the inhabitants, especially those who, like myself, lived through the war and the separation of brothers and sisters belonging to the same nation because of destructive and inhuman ideologies that, beneath a mask of dreams and illusions, burdened men and women with the heavy yoke of oppression. Thus, you will understand that I am particularly sensitive to dialogue between all human beings in order to overcome every kind of conflict and tension and to make our earth an earth of peace and brotherhood.

All together, by combining their efforts, Christian communities, national leaders, diplomats, and all people of good will are called to achieve a peaceful society, to overcome the temptation of confrontation between cultures, races, and worlds that are different. For this, each people must find in its spiritual and cultural patrimony the best values it possesses so that it may advance undaunted to encounter the other, ready to share its own spiritual and material riches for the benefit of all.

In order to continue in this direction, the Church never ceases to proclaim and defend the fundamental human rights, which unfortunately are still violated in various parts of the earth. She is working for recognition of the rights of every human person to life, food, a home, work, health-care assistance, the protection of the family and the promotion of social development, with respect for the dignity of men and of women, created in the image of God.

Rest assured that the Catholic Church will continue to offer to cooperate, in her own province and with her own means, to safeguard the dignity of every person and to serve the common good. She asks no privileges for herself but only the legitimate conditions of freedom to carry out her mission. In the concert of nations, she always seeks to encourage understanding and cooperation between peoples based on loyalty, discretion, and friendliness.

ADDRESS TO THE DIPLOMATIC CORPS ACCREDITED
TO THE HOLY SEE, MAY 12, 2005

Catholics Throughout the World

We have seen how, in Rome, Africa is present, India is present, the universe is present. And this presence of our brothers and sisters obliges us to think not only of ourselves, but to feel precisely in this moment of history, in all of these circumstances with which we are familiar, the presence of the other continents.

It seems to me that at this time we have a particular responsibility towards Africa, towards Latin America, and towards Asia, where Christianity—with the exception of the Philippines—is still a very large minority, even if in India it is growing and shows itself a strength for the future.

ADDRESS TO THE CLERGY OF ROME, MAY 13, 2005

Breaking Down Barriers

The Church must always become anew what she already is; she must open the borders between peoples and break down the barriers between class and race. In her, there cannot be those who are forgotten or looked down upon. In the Church there are only free brothers and sisters of Jesus Christ. The wind and fire of the Holy Spirit must continually break down those barriers that we men and women continue to build between us; we must continually pass from Babel—being closed in on ourselves—to Pentecost.

PENTECOST SUNDAY HOMILY, MAY 15, 2005

Dialogue Between Cultures

*T*ragically, cultural differences have often been a source of misunderstanding between peoples and even the cause of senseless conflicts and wars. In fact dialogue between cultures is an indispensable building stone of the universal civilization of love for which every man and woman longs. I encourage you and your citizens therefore to affirm the fundamental values common to all cultures; common because they find their source in the very nature of the human person. In this way the quest for peace is consolidated allowing you to dedicate every human and spiritual resource to the material and moral progress of your people, in a spirit of fruitful co-operation with neighboring countries....

The people...have already achieved much

in the difficult but rewarding task of ensuring social coherence and stability. Authentic development requires a coordinated national plan of progress which honors the legitimate aspirations of all sectors of society and to which political and civic leaders can be held accountable. Human history teaches us repeatedly that if such programs are to effect a lasting positive change, they must be based on the protection of human rights including those of ethnic and religious minorities, the practice of responsible and transparent governance, and the maintenance of law and order by an impartial judiciary system and an honorable police force. Without these foundations, the hope for true progress remains elusive.

ADDRESS TO THE AMBASSADOR OF THE FORMER
YUGOSLAV REPUBLIC OF MACEDONIA, MAY 19, 2005

Cultural Preparation for Salvation

The mission of the Church is not in conflict with respect for other religious and cultural traditions. Christ takes nothing away from man; rather, he gives fullness of life, joy, and hope. Of this hope, you are also called to "give reason" (1 Peter 3:15) in the different settings where Providence will destine you.

To carry out adequately the service that awaits you and that the Church entrusts to you, a solid cultural preparation is necessary, which includes the knowledge of languages, of history and of law, with wise openness to different cultures. It then becomes necessary that, at an even deeper level, you propose holiness and the salvation of the souls that you meet on your journey as the fundamental aim of your existence.

ADDRESS TO THE PRIESTS OF THE PONTIFICAL ECCLESIASTICAL ACADEMY, MAY 20, 2005

The Roots of Shared Values

I am convinced that the way to give life to a society truly attentive to the common good is to seek in the Gospel the roots of shared values....This is the ardent desire of the Catholic Church which has no other interest but to spread and bear witness to Jesus Christ's words of hope and love, words of life which down the centuries have inspired many martyrs and confessors of the faith.

ADDRESS TO THE PRIME MINISTER OF THE FORMER YUGOSLAV REPUBLIC OF MACEDONIA, MAY 23, 2005

Mobilizing the Spirit

To proclaim the Gospel's liberating newness to every human person, to reach out to him in all that makes up his life and expresses his humanity, is the Church's ongoing challenge. This mission, received by the Church from her Lord, basically corresponds with your initiative [Colloquium on "Culture, Reason, and Freedom"] and highly justifies the desire that the Holy See has always had to take part, through the presence of a Permanent Observer, in your reflections and commitment. This is what the Catholic Church will continue to do, mobilizing her own forces which are first and foremost spiritual, to contribute to the good of human beings in all the dimensions of their being.

In a world at the same time many-faceted and enlightened but also subjected to the pressing demands of the globalization of economic relations and especially of information, it is of the utmost importance to mobilize the energies of intelligence so that the human person's right to education and culture may be recognized everywhere, particularly in the poorest countries.

In this world where men and women must learn increasingly to recognize and respect their brothers and sisters, the Church wants to make her own contribution to serving the human community by shedding more and more light on the relationship that unites each person to the Creator of all life and is the basis of the inalienable dignity of every human being, from conception to natural death.

LETTER TO CARDINAL JEAN-LOUIS TAURAN ON THE OCCASION OF THE COLLOQUIUM "CULTURE, REASON AND FREEDOM," MAY 24, 2005

Witness to Christ in Today's Society

The kind of culture that is based on a purely functional rationality which contradicts and seeks to exclude Christianity, and the religious and moral traditions of humanity in general, is of course as present and active in Italy as it is more or less everywhere in Europe.

Here, however, its supremacy is not total, nor, still less, is there any lack of opposition to it. Indeed, many people, even those who do not share or at any rate do not practice our faith, feel that such a form of culture is actually a harmful mutilation of man and of his reasoning.

….[T]he Church has a far-reaching network among people of every age and condition; thus, she can propose the message of salvation that the Lord has entrusted to her in the most varied situations....

The domain of culture is undoubtedly crucial for the future of the faith and the general orientation of a nation's life. I therefore ask you to persevere in the work you have undertaken so that the voice of Catholics may be constantly present and, especially, to reinforce the ability to work out rationally, in the light of faith, the many questions that are surfacing in the various contexts of knowledge and in the great decisions of life.

Culture and behavioral models today are increasingly conditioned and influenced by images presented by the media. Thus, ...[the] efforts to establish also in this context an adequate means of expression in order to offer to all a Christian interpretation of events and problems deserve praise....

As my beloved predecessor John Paul II frequently emphasized, Italy can and must play an important role in the common witness to Jesus Christ, our one Savior, so that the standard of true humanism may be identified with Christ, in the people's conscience and the whole ordering of social life.

ADDRESS TO THE ITALIAN BISHOPS, MAY 30, 2005

In the Service of All Nations

The noble goal of attaining the common good through an ordered social life can only be attained if political leaders are devoted to ensuring the welfare of individuals and groups in a spirit of integrity and fairness....

...Through her network of educational institutions, hospitals, dispensaries, and orphanages, the Church stands at the service of people of all religions. She seeks to offer a specific contribution to the future of the nation by educating people in the practical skills and the spiritual values which will serve as the foundation for social renewal. For her part, the Church asks only for the freedom to carry out her proper mission, which serves the coming of God's Kingdom through her prophetic witness to the Gospel and her inculcation of its moral teaching. The Church thus works for the building of a harmonious and just society, while at the same time respecting and encouraging the freedom and responsibility of citizens to participate in the political process and in the pursuit of the common good.

ADDRESS TO THE AMBASSADOR OF THE
REPUBLIC OF ZIMBABWE, JUNE 16, 2005

The Dignity of the Human Person

$\mathcal{S}$ound economic development has been a long-standing aspiration of all....It is also a right which carries the corresponding duty to contribute, according to one's ability, to the genuine progress of the community. The priority of promoting social and commercial projects capable of creating a more equitable society represents a difficult though stimulating challenge for all who regulate and work in the business sector.

...Only in respecting the inviolable dignity of the human person and promoting the corresponding individual liberties can a civil society be constructed which contributes to the prosperity of all its citizens.

ADDRESS TO THE AMBASSADOR OF THE
REPUBLIC OF AZERBAIJAN, JUNE 16, 2005

Creating Community

Our world is facing numerous challenges that it must successfully confront so that the human person may always triumph over technology. A just future for peoples must be the primary concern of those who have undertaken to manage public affairs, not in their own interest but with a view to the common good. Our heart cannot be at peace while we see our brothers and sisters suffering from lack of food, work, a home, or the other fundamental goods.

To make a concrete response to the appeal of our brothers and sisters in humanity, we must come to grips with the first of these challenges: solidarity among generations, solidarity between countries and entire continents, so that all human beings may share more equitably in the riches of our planet. This is one of the essential services that people of good will must render to humanity. The earth, in fact, can produce enough to nourish all its inhabitants, on the condition that the rich countries do not keep for themselves what belongs to all.

The Church will never tire of reminding everyone that they must take pains to create a human brotherhood that consists of concrete gestures on the part of individuals and of governments and international institutions.

For her part, having made sharing the heart of her life since apostolic times, the Church will continue on all the continents to go to the aid of their populations with the support of the local communities and of all people of good will, especially in the areas of education, health care, and the basic goods. I know that as diplomats, you are particularly sensitive to this aspect of life in society and that diplomacy has an important role to play.

ADDRESS AT THE PRESENTATION OF THE
LETTERS ACCREDITING NEW AMBASSADORS
TO THE HOLY SEE, JUNE 16, 2005

CHRISTIAN UNITY: PEACE FOR THE HUMAN FAMILY

Purification of Memory

With full awareness, therefore, at the beginning of his ministry in the Church of Rome which Peter bathed in his blood, Peter's current successor takes on as his primary task the duty to work tirelessly to rebuild the full and visible unity of all Christ's followers. This is his ambition, his impelling duty. He is aware that good intentions do not suffice for this. Concrete gestures that enter hearts and stir consciences are essential, inspiring in everyone that inner conversion that is the prerequisite for all ecumenical progress.

Theological dialogue is necessary; the investigation of the historical reasons for the decisions made in the past is also indispensable. But what is most urgently needed is that "purification of memory," so often recalled by John Paul II, which alone can dispose souls to accept the full truth of Christ. Each one of us must come before him, the supreme Judge of every living person, and render an account to him of all we have done or have failed to do to further the great good of the full and visible unity of all his disciples.

The current successor of Peter is allowing himself to be called in the first person by this requirement and is prepared to do everything in his power to promote the fundamental cause of ecumenism. Following the example of his predecessors, he is fully determined to encourage every initiative that seems appropriate for promoting contacts and understanding with the representatives of the different Churches and Ecclesial Communities....

The Church of today must revive her awareness of the duty to re-propose to the world the voice of the One who said: "I am the light of the world. No follower of mine shall ever walk in darkness; no, he shall possess the light of life" (John 8:12). In carrying out his ministry, the new pope knows that his task is to make Christ's light shine out before the men and women of today: not his own light, but Christ's....

I ask God for unity and peace for the human family, and declare the willingness of all Catholics to cooperate for an authentic social development, respectful of the dignity of every human being.

I will make every conscientious effort to continue the promising dialogue initiated by my venerable predecessors with the different civilizations, so that mutual understanding may create the conditions for a better future for all.

First Message of Pope Benedict XVI,
April 20, 2005

The Sacrament of Unity

I feel it my duty, in the first place, to thank God who wanted me, despite my human frailty, as the successor of the Apostle Peter, and has entrusted to me the task of governing and guiding the Church so that she may be the sacrament of unity in the world for the entire human race (*Lumen Gentium*, n. 1).

ADDRESS TO THE MEMBERS OF THE
COLLEGE OF CARDINALS, APRIL 22, 2005

The Shepherd and the Fisherman

*B*oth the image of the shepherd and that of the fisherman issue an explicit call to unity. "I have other sheep that are not of this fold; I must lead them too, and they will heed my voice. So there shall be one flock, one shepherd" (John 10:16); these are the words of Jesus at the end of his discourse on the Good Shepherd. And the account of the 153 large fish ends with the joyful statement: "although there were so many, the net was not torn" (John 21:11). Alas, beloved Lord, with sorrow we must now acknowledge that it has been torn! But no—we must not be sad! Let us rejoice because of your promise, which does not disappoint, and let us do all we can to pursue the path towards the unity you have promised. Let us remember it in our prayer to the Lord, as we plead with him: yes, Lord, remember your promise. Grant that we may be one flock and one shepherd! Do not allow your net to be torn, help us to be servants of unity!

HOMILY AT THE IMPOSITION OF THE PALLIUM AND CONFERRAL OF THE FISHERMAN'S RING, APRIL 24, 2005

That They May All Be One

I would like to thank the Lord who has blessed us with his mercy and instilled in us sincere willingness to make his prayer our own: *ut unum sint* ["that they may all be one" (John 17:21)]. He has thus made us increasingly aware of the importance of moving forward towards full communion. With brotherly friendship we can exchange the gifts we have received from the Spirit, and we feel urged to encourage one another so that we may proclaim Christ and his message to the world, which often appears troubled and restless, uninformed and indifferent.

…Let us go forward with hope. In the footsteps of my predecessors, especially Paul VI and John Paul II, I feel strongly the need to reassert the irreversible commitment taken by the Second Vatican Council and pursued in recent years—also thanks to the activity of the Pontifical Council for Promoting Christian Unity. The path to the full communion desired by Jesus for his disciples entails, with true docility to what the Spirit says to the Churches, courage, gentleness, firmness and hope, in order to reach our goal. Above all, it requires persistent prayer and with one heart, in order to obtain from the Good Shepherd the gift of unity for his flock.

[J]oin with me in setting an example of that spiritual ecumenism which, through prayer, can bring about our communion without obstacles.

…The world in which we live is often marked by conflicts, violence, and war, but it earnestly longs for peace, peace which is above all a gift from God, peace for which we must pray without ceasing. Yet peace is also a duty to which all peoples must be committed, especially those who profess to belong to religious traditions. Our efforts to come together and foster dialogue are a valuable contribution to building peace on solid foundations. Pope John Paul II, my venerable predecessor, wrote at the start of the new millennium that "the name of the one God must become increasingly what it is: a name of peace and a summons to peace" (*Novo Millennio Ineunte*, 55). It is therefore imperative to engage in authentic and sincere dialogue, built on respect for the dignity of every human person, created, as we Christians firmly believe, in the image and likeness of God (Genesis 1:26–27).

ADDRESS TO THE DELEGATES OF OTHER CHURCHES AND ECCLESIAL COMMUNITIES AND OTHER RELIGIOUS TRADITIONS, APRIL 25, 2005

The Path to Full Communion

I would like to greet with particular affection the Orthodox Churches, the Oriental Orthodox Churches, and those Oriental Catholic Churches that are celebrating Christ's Resurrection on this very Sunday. I address to these beloved brothers and sisters of ours the traditional proclamation of joy: *Christos anesti!* Yes, Christ is risen, he is truly risen. I hope with all my heart that the celebration of Easter may be for them a unanimous prayer of faith and praise to the One who is our common Lord and is calling us to walk with determination on the path that leads to full communion.

REGINA CAELI, MAY 1, 2005

The Wind and Fire of the Spirit

The Church must always become anew what she already is; she must open the borders between peoples and break down the barriers between class and race. In her, there cannot be those who are forgotten or looked down upon. In the Church there are only free brothers and sisters of Jesus Christ. The wind and fire of the Holy Spirit must continually break down those barriers that we men and women continue to build between us; we must continually pass from Babel—being closed in on ourselves—to Pentecost.

Thus, we must continually pray that the Holy Spirit opens us and gives us the grace of understanding, so that we become the People of God deriving from all peoples. Saint Paul tells us more along these lines: in Christ, who as the one Bread feeds all of us in the Eucharist and draws us to him in his Body wracked on the cross, we must become only one body and one spirit.

HOMILY AT THE MASS OF
PRIESTLY ORDINATION, MAY 15, 2005

Unity in the Upper Room

The Eucharist…is the sacrament of unity. Unfortunately, however, Christians are divided, precisely in the sacrament of unity. Sustained by the Eucharist, we must feel all the more roused to strive with all our strength for that full unity which Christ ardently desired in the Upper Room.

HOMILY AT THE 24TH ITALIAN NATIONAL
EUCHARISTIC CONGRESS, MAY 29, 2005

Stirring the Heart and Conscience

Relations between the Catholic Church and the World Council [of Churches] developed during the Second Vatican Council, where two observers from Geneva were present at all four sessions. This led in 1965 to the establishment of the Joint Working Group as an instrument of ongoing contact and cooperation, which would keep in mind the common task of unity in answer to the Lord's own prayer, "that they may all be one" (John 17:21). Next November an important consultation on the future of the Joint Working

Group will be held to mark the fortieth anniversary of its founding. My hope and prayer is that its purpose and working methodology will be further clarified for the sake of ever more effective ecumenical understanding, cooperation and progress.

In the very first days of my pontificate I stated that my "primary task is the duty to work tirelessly to rebuild the full and visible unity of all Christ's followers." This requires, in addition to good intentions, "concrete gestures which enter hearts and stir consciences…inspiring in everyone that inner conversion that is the prerequisite for all ecumenical progress" (*Missa Pro Ecclesia*, 5).

Pope John Paul II often recalled that the heart of the search for Christian unity is "spiritual ecumenism." He saw its core in terms of being in Christ: "To believe in Christ means to desire unity; to desire unity means to desire the Church; to desire the Church means to desire the communion of grace which corresponds to the Father's plan from all eternity. Such is the meaning of Christ's prayer: "*Ut unum sint*" (Encyclical Letter, *Ut Unum Sint*, 9).

ADDRESS TO MEMBERS OF THE DELEGATION FROM THE WORLD COUNCIL OF CHURCHES, JUNE 16, 2005

One, Holy, Catholic, and Apostolic

If it is true that the Lord calls with force his disciples to build unity in charity and truth; if it is true that the ecumenical appeal is a pressing invitation to rebuild, in reconciliation and peace, the unity, seriously damaged, of all Christians; if we cannot ignore that division makes the holy cause of proclaiming the Gospel to every person less efficient, how can we avoid the duty of examining with clarity and good will our differences?...

The unity we seek is neither absorption nor fusion but respect for the multiform fullness of the Church which, conformed to the will of her founder Jesus Christ, must always be one, holy, catholic, and apostolic.

ADDRESS TO THE ECUMENICAL PATRIARCH OF CONSTANTINOPLE, JUNE 30, 2005

EUCHARIST:
THE SOURCE OF
THE CHURCH'S
MISSION

The Heart of Christian Life

My pontificate begins in a particularly meaningful way as the Church is living the special year dedicated to the Eucharist. How could I fail to see this providential coincidence as an element that must mark the ministry to which I am called? The Eucharist, the heart of Christian life and the source of the Church's evangelizing mission, cannot but constitute the permanent center and source of the Petrine ministry that has been entrusted to me.

The Eucharist makes constantly present the Risen Christ who continues to give himself to us, calling us to participate in the banquet of his Body and his Blood. From full communion with him flows every other element of the Church's life: first of all, communion among all the faithful, the commitment to proclaiming and witnessing to the Gospel, the ardor of love for all, especially the poorest and lowliest.

...I ask everyone in the coming months to intensify love and devotion for Jesus in the Eucharist, and to express courageously and clearly faith in the Real Presence of the Lord, especially by the solemnity and the correctness of the celebrations.

I ask this especially of priests, whom I am thinking of with deep affection at this moment. The ministerial priesthood was born at the Last Supper, together with the Eucharist, as my venerable predecessor John Paul II so frequently emphasized. "All the more then must the life of a priest be 'shaped' by the Eucharist" (Letter to Priests for Holy Thursday 2005, n. 1). In the first place, the devout, daily celebration of holy Mass, the center of the life and mission of every priest, contributes to this goal.

Nourished and sustained by the Eucharist, Catholics cannot but feel encouraged to strive for the full unity for which Christ expressed so ardent a hope in the Upper Room. The successor of Peter knows that he must make himself especially responsible for his Divine Master's supreme aspiration. Indeed, he is entrusted with the task of strengthening his brethren (Luke 22:32).

FIRST MESSAGE OF POPE BENEDICT XVI,
APRIL 20, 2005

Agape

For the ancient Church, the word "love," *agape*, referred to the mystery of the Eucharist. In this mystery, Christ's love becomes permanently tangible among us. Here, again and again he gives himself. Here, again and again his heart is pierced; here he keeps his promise, the promise which, from the cross, was to attract all things to himself.

In the Eucharist, we ourselves learn Christ's love. It was thanks to this center and heart, thanks to the Eucharist, that the saints lived, bringing to the world God's love in ever new ways and forms. Thanks to the Eucharist, the Church is reborn ever anew! The Church is none other than that network—the eucharistic community—within which all of us, receiving the same Lord, become one body and embrace the entire world.

Presiding in doctrine and presiding in love must in the end be one and the same: the whole of the Church's teaching leads ultimately to love. And the Eucharist, as the love of Jesus Christ present, is the criterion for all teaching. On love the whole law is based, and the prophets as well, the Lord says (see Matthew

22:40). Love is the fulfillment of the law, Saint Paul wrote to the Romans (see Romans 13:10).

HOMILY AT THE MASS OF POSSESSION OF THE CHAIR OF THE BISHOP OF ROME, MAY 7, 2005

Nourishment and Sustenance

Catholics of the entire world are encouraged to renew their understanding of the great gift given to us by Christ at the Last Supper. In the bread and in the wine, which in the holy Mass become the Body and Blood of the Lord, may the Christian people find nourishment and sustenance to travel on the path towards sanctity, the universal vocation of all the baptized.

I count on being present…to render homage to Christ in the sacrament of his love and at the same time to reinforce the ties of communion that bind the successor of Peter to the Church….

LETTER TO CARDINAL CAMILLO RUINI, MAY 13, 2005

Ministers of Peace

To each one of you [candidates for ordination], in a very personal way, the Lord says: "Peace to [all of] you—peace to you!" When the Lord says this, he does not give something, but he gives himself. Indeed, he himself is peace (see Ephesians 2:14).

In this greeting of the Lord, we can also foresee a reference to the great mystery of faith, to the holy Eucharist, in which he continually gives himself to us, and, in this way, true peace.

This greeting is placed at the center of your priestly mission: the Lord entrusts to you the mystery of this sacrament. In his name you can say: "This is my Body....This is my Blood." Allow yourselves to be drawn ever anew by the holy Eucharist, by communion of life with Christ. Consider the center of each day the possibility to celebrate the Eucharist worthily. Lead people ever anew to this mystery. Help them, starting from this, to bring the peace of Christ into the world.

HOMILY AT THE MASS OF
PRIESTLY ORDINATION, MAY 15, 2005

God Is Love

In the light of the Pascal Mystery, the center of the universe and of history is fully revealed: God himself, eternal and infinite Love. The word that summarizes all revelation is this: "God is love" (1 John 4:8, 16); and love is always a mystery, a reality that surpasses reason without contradicting it, and more than that, exalts its possibilities.

Jesus revealed to us the mystery of God: he, the Son, made us know the Father who is in heaven, and gave us the Holy Spirit, the love of the Father and of the Son. Christian theology synthesizes the truth of God with this expression: only one substance in three Persons. God is not solitude, but perfect communion. For this reason the human person, the image of God, realizes himself or herself in love, which is a sincere gift of self.

We are contemplating the mystery of the love of God shared in a sublime way in the most holy Eucharist, the sacrament of the Body and Blood of Christ, the representation of his redeeming sacrifice.

...In the heart of this year dedicated to the Eucharist, the Christian people converge around Christ present in the most holy sacrament, the source and summit of their life and mission.

In particular, each parish is called to rediscover the beauty of Sunday, the Lord's Day, in which the disciples of Christ renew, in the Eucharist, communion with the One who gives meaning to the joys and hardships of each day.

"Without Sunday we cannot live" [This was the theme for the Italian National Eucharistic Congress]. This is what the first Christians professed, even at the cost of their lives, and this is what we are called to repeat today.

ANGELUS, MAY 22, 2005

The Intimate Mystery

By faith, the Eucharist is an intimate mystery. The Lord instituted the sacrament in the Upper Room, surrounded by his new family, by the Twelve Apostles, a prefiguring and anticipation of the Church of all times.

And so, in the liturgy of the ancient Church, the distribution of holy Communion was introduced with the words *Sancta sanctis*: the holy gift is intended for those who have been made holy.

In this way a response was given to the exhortation of Saint Paul to the Corinthians: "A man should examine himself first; only then should he eat of the bread and drink of the cup..." (1 Corinthians 11:28).

Nevertheless, from this intimacy that is a most personal gift of the Lord, the strength of the sacrament of the Eucharist goes above and beyond the walls of our churches. In this sacrament, the Lord is always journeying to meet the world....

[Through the liturgical procession of *Corpus Domini*] [w]e bring Christ, present under the sign of bread, onto the streets of our city. We entrust these streets, these homes, our daily life, to his goodness. May our streets be streets of Jesus! May our houses be homes for him and with him! May our life of every day be penetrated by his presence.

With this gesture, let us place under his eyes the sufferings of the sick, the solitude of young people and the elderly, temptations, fears—our entire life....

It is not possible to "eat" the Risen One, present under the sign of bread, as if it were a simple piece of bread. To eat this Bread is to communicate, to enter into communion with the person of the living Lord. This communion, this act of "eating," is truly an encounter between two persons; it is allowing our lives to be penetrated by the life of the One who is the Lord, of the One who is my Creator and Redeemer.

The purpose of this communion, of this partaking, is the assimilation of my life with his, my transformation and conformation into he who is living Love. Therefore, this communion implies adoration; it implies the will to follow Christ, to follow the One who goes ahead of us. Adoration and procession thereby make up a single gesture of communion; they answer his mandate: "Take and eat."

HOMILY FOR THE SOLEMNITY OF
CORPUS DOMINI, MAY 26, 2005

Bread From Heaven

It is not easy for us to live as Christians.... From a spiritual point of view, the world in which we find ourselves, often marked by unbridled consumerism, religious indifference and a secularism closed to transcendence, can appear a desert just as "vast and terrible" as the one...from the Book of Deuteronomy (8:15). God came to the aid of the Jewish people in difficulty in this desert with his gift of manna, to make them understand that "not by bread alone does man live, but by every word that comes forth from the mouth of the Lord" (Deuteronomy 8:3).

...Jesus has explained to us, through the gift of manna, for what bread God wanted to prepare the people of the New Covenant. Alluding to the Eucharist he said: "This is the bread that came down from heaven. Unlike your ancestors who ate and died nonetheless, the man who feeds on this bread shall live forever" (John 6:58).

In taking flesh, the Son of God could become Bread and thus be the nourishment of his people, of us, journeying on in this world towards the promised land of heaven....

"He who feeds on my flesh and drinks my blood remains in me, and I in him" (John 6:56). How is it possible not to rejoice in such a promise?...

Christ is truly present among us in the Eucharist. His presence is not static. It is a dynamic presence that grasps us, to make us his own, to make us assimilate him. Christ draws us to him, he makes us come out of ourselves to make us all one with him. In this way he also integrates us in the communities of brothers and sisters, and communion with the Lord is always also communion with our brothers and sisters. And we see the beauty of this communion that the blessed Eucharist gives us.

HOMILY AT CLOSING OF THE 24TH ITALIAN NATIONAL EUCHARISTIC CONGRESS, MAY 29, 2005

Caring for the Liturgy

It is true: our spiritual life essentially depends upon the Eucharist. Without it, faith and hope are extinguished and charity cools.

This is why, dear friends, I urge you to take better and better care of the quality of the eucharistic celebrations, especially those on Sunday, so that Sunday may truly be the Lord's Day and confer fullness of meaning on everyday events and activities, demonstrating the joy and beauty of the faith.

ADDRESS TO PILGRIMS FROM THE DIOCESE OF VERONA IN NORTHERN ITALY, JUNE 4, 2005

Nourishment to Serve

The loving attention of Christians to those in difficulty and their commitment to a more supportive society are continually nourished by active and conscious participation in the Eucharist. Anyone nourished with the faith of Christ at the eucharistic table assimilates his same style of life, which is the style of service especially attentive to the weakest and most underprivileged persons. In fact, practical charity is a criterion that proves the authenticity of our liturgical celebrations (see Apostolic Letter *Mane Nobiscum Domine*, n. 28).

May the Year of the Eucharist which we are living in help the diocesan and parish communities to revive this capacity of going out to relieve the many forms of poverty in our world.

Angelus, June 19, 2005

The Hour of Jesus

At the celebration of the Eucharist, we find ourselves in the "hour" of Jesus, to use the language of John's Gospel. Through the Eucharist this "hour" of Jesus becomes our own hour, his presence in our midst. Together with the disciples he celebrated the Passover of Israel, the memorial of God's liberating action that led Israel from slavery to freedom. Jesus follows the rites of Israel. He recites over the bread the prayer of praise and blessing. But then something new happens. He thanks God not only for the great works of the past; he thanks him for his own exaltation, soon to be accomplished through the cross and Resurrection, and he speaks to the disciples in words that sum up the whole of the Law and the Prophets: "This is my Body, given in sacrifice for you. This cup is the New Covenant in my Blood." He then distributes the bread and the cup, and instructs them to repeat his words and actions of that moment over and over again in his memory.

Jesus did not instruct us to repeat the Passover meal, which in any event, given that it is an anniversary, is not repeatable at will. He instructed us to enter into his "hour." We enter into it through the sacred power of the words of consecration—a transformation brought about through the prayer of praise which places us in continuity with Israel and the whole of salvation history, and at the same time ushers in the new, to which the older prayer at its deepest level was pointing. The new prayer—which the Church calls the "Eucharistic Prayer"—brings the Eucharist into being. It is the word of power which transforms the gifts of the earth in an entirely new way into God's gift of himself and it draws us into this process of transformation. That is why we call this action "Eucharist," which is a translation of the Hebrew word *beracha*—thanksgiving, praise, blessing, and a transformation worked by the Lord: the presence of his "hour." Jesus' hour is the hour in which love triumphs. In other words: it is God who has triumphed, because he is Love. Jesus' hour seeks to become our own hour and will indeed become so if we allow ourselves, through the celebration of the Eucharist, to be drawn into that process of transformation that the Lord intends to bring about. The Eucharist must become the center of our lives.

HOMILY AT THE 20TH WORLD YOUTH DAY,
AUGUST 21, 2005

Becoming the Body of Christ

The Body and Blood of Christ are given to us so that we ourselves will be transformed in our turn. We are to become the Body of Christ, his own flesh and blood. We all eat the one bread, and this means that we ourselves become one. In this way, adoration, as we said earlier, becomes union. God no longer simply stands before us, as the one who is totally

Other. He is within us, and we are in him. His dynamic enters into us and then seeks to spread outwards to others until it fills the world, so that his love can truly become the dominant measure of the world....

HOMILY AT THE 20TH WORLD YOUTH DAY,
AUGUST 21, 2005

Pledge Your Love

The Eucharist releases the joy that we need so much, and we must learn to grasp it ever more deeply, we must learn to love it. Let us pledge ourselves to do this—it is worth the effort! Let us discover the intimate riches of the Church's liturgy and its true greatness: it is not we who are celebrating for ourselves, but it is the living God himself who is preparing a banquet for us.

HOMILY AT THE 20TH WORLD YOUTH DAY,
AUGUST 21, 2005

One With Our Neighbors

Because there is one bread, we, though many, are one body," says Saint Paul (1 Corinthians 10:17). By this he meant: since we receive the same Lord and he gathers us together and draws us into himself, we ourselves are one. This must be evident in our lives. It must be seen in our capacity to forgive. It must be seen in our sensitivity to the needs of others. It must be seen in our willingness to share. It must be seen in our commitment to our neighbors, both those close at hand and those physically far away, whom we nevertheless consider to be close.

HOMILY AT THE 20TH WORLD YOUTH DAY,
AUGUST 21, 2005

ℳINISTRY:
SERVING
LIKE CHRIST

Servant of the Servants of God

$\mathcal{I}$ am preparing to undertake this special ministry, the "Petrine" ministry at the service of the universal Church, with humble abandonment into the hands of God's providence. I first of all renew my total and confident loyalty to Christ: *In Te, Domine, speravi; non confundar in aeternum!* ["O Lord, in you I have put my trust; let me never be put to shame." This phrase—taken from Psalm 70–71, and often associated with the *Te Deum*—was the motto of Pope Benedict XV (1914–1922), the "Pope of Peace"].

Your Eminences [members of the College of Cardinals], with heartfelt gratitude for the trust you have shown me, I ask you to support me with your prayers and with your constant, active and wise collaboration. I also ask all my Brothers in the Episcopate to be close to me with their prayers and advice, so that I may truly be the *Servus servorum Dei* ["Servant of the servants of God"—a phrase that has been used to describe the office of the papacy since Pope Gregory the Great (590–604)].

ADDRESS TO THE MEMBERS OF THE COLLEGE OF CARDINALS, APRIL 20, 2005

Unconditional Service

Mane nobiscum, Domine! "Stay with us, Lord!" This invocation, which is the principal topic of the Apostolic Letter of John Paul II for the Year of the Eucharist, is the prayer that wells up spontaneously from my heart as I prepare to begin the ministry to which Christ has called me. Like Peter, I too renew to him my unconditional promise of fidelity. I intend to serve him alone, dedicating myself totally to the service of his Church.

ADDRESS TO THE MEMBERS OF THE COLLEGE OF CARDINALS, APRIL 20, 2005

In the Service of the Church

If on the one hand I am aware of my personal limitations and limited abilities, on the other hand I well know the nature of the mission entrusted to me and am preparing myself to carry it out with an attitude of inner dedication. It is not a matter of honors but of a service to be rendered with simplicity and willingness, imitating our Teacher and Lord who did not come to be served but to serve (see Matthew 20:28), and at the Last Supper washed the apostles' feet, commanding them to do likewise (see John 13:13–14). It only remains for me—and for all of us together—to accept from Providence the will of God and to do our best to measure up to it, helping one another to carry out our respective tasks in the service of the Church.

ADDRESS TO THE MEMBERS OF THE COLLEGE OF CARDINALS, APRIL 22, 2005

Feed My Sheep

The lamb's wool [of the pope's Pallium] is meant to represent the lost, sick, or weak sheep which the shepherd places on his shoulders and carries to the waters of life. For the Fathers of the Church, the parable of the lost sheep, which the shepherd seeks in the desert, was an image of the mystery of Christ and the Church. The human race—every one of us—is the sheep lost in the desert which no longer knows the way. The Son of God will not let this happen; he cannot abandon humanity in so wretched a condition. He leaps to his feet and abandons the glory of heaven, in order to go in search of the sheep and pursue it, all the way to the cross. He takes it upon his shoulders and carries our humanity; he carries us all—he is the good shepherd who lays down his life for the sheep. What the Pallium indicates first and foremost is that we are all carried by Christ. But at the same time it invites us to carry one another.

…When the shepherd of all humanity, the living God, himself became a lamb, he stood on the side of the lambs, with those who are downtrodden and killed. This is how he reveals himself to be the true shepherd: "I am the Good Shepherd…I lay down my life for the sheep," Jesus says of himself (John 10:14 ff.).

One of the basic characteristics of a shepherd must be to love the people entrusted to him, even as he loves Christ whom he serves. "Feed my sheep," says Christ to Peter, and now, at this moment, he says it to me as well. Feeding means loving, and loving also means being ready to suffer. Loving means giving the sheep what is truly good, the nourishment of God's truth, of God's word, the nourishment of his presence, which he gives us in the Blessed Sacrament.

IMPOSITION OF THE PALLIUM AND CONFERRAL OF THE FISHERMAN'S RING, APRIL 24, 2005

Truth, Justice, and the Good

When he [Jesus Christ] speaks of the cross that we ourselves have to carry, it has nothing to do with a taste for torture or of pedantic moralism. It is the impulse of love, which has its own momentum and does not seek itself but opens the person to the service of truth, justice, and the good. Christ shows God to us, and thus the true greatness of man.

INAUGURATION CEREMONY OF THE
PONTIFICATE, APRIL 25, 2005

Mandate to Serve

The power that Christ conferred upon Peter and his successors is, in an absolute sense, a mandate to serve. The power of teaching in the Church involves a commitment to the service of obedience to the faith. The pope is not an absolute monarch whose thoughts and desires are law. On the contrary: the pope's ministry is a guarantee of obedience to Christ and to his Word. He must not proclaim his own ideas, but rather constantly bind himself and the Church to obedience to God's Word, in the

face of every attempt to adapt it or water it
down, and every form of opportunism.

HOMILY DURING MASS OF POSSESSION
OF THE CHAIR OF THE BISHOP OF ROME, MAY 7, 2005

Serving Our Sister Churches

Thus, humbly attached to Christ, our One
Lord, together we can and must encourage that
"exemplarity" of the Church of Rome which is
genuine service to our Sister Churches across
the world. The indissoluble bond between
romanum and *petrinum* implies and indeed
requires the Church of Rome's participation in
the universal concern of her Bishops.

ADDRESS TO THE CLERGY OF ROME, MAY 13, 2005

The Living Presence of Jesus

We welcome Jesus' living presence in
ourselves to bring him to everyone by loving
service.

ANGELUS, MAY 29, 2005

Simplicity, Chastity, and Humble Service

*P*riestly identity must never be likened to any secular title or confused with civic or political office. Rather, configured to Christ who emptied himself taking the form of a servant (see Philippians 2:7–8), the priest lives a life of simplicity, chastity and humble service, which inspires others by example.

ADDRESS TO THE BISHOPS OF THE EPISCOPAL CONFERENCE OF PAPUA NEW GUINEA AND SOLOMON ISLANDS, JUNE 25, 2005

Authentic Peace in Society

*Y*ou are Peter, and on this rock I will build my church" (Matthew 16:18). Jesus addresses Peter with these words after his profession of faith. He was the same disciple who was later to deny Christ. So why is Peter described as "rock"?

Certainly not because of his personal solidity. "Rock" is rather a *nomen officii:* in other words, not a title of merit but of service, which defines a calling and a responsibility of divine origin for which no one is equipped simply by virtue of his own character.

Peter, foundering, who sank in the waters of the Lake of Tiberias, becomes the rock on which the divine Master built his Church. This is the faith that you want to reaffirm by renewing your attachment to the successor of Peter....

Persevere, dear friends, each one in your own province and in accordance with your own possibilities, in offering your collaboration for the safeguard of the dignity of every person, for the defense of human life in the service of a determined action of authentic peace in every social milieu.

ADDRESS TO MEMBERS OF THE DON ORIONE FAMILY,
JUNE 28, 2005

Service to the Suffering

The Church is making us understand that service to the suffering and the defense of life are vocations with a deep religious dimension and that there are forms [of consecrated and lay life] in which to live such vocations.

ADDRESS TO DIOCESAN CLERGY OF AOSTA,
JULY 25, 2005

Institutions That Serve

The Catholic Church maintains a presence in public life through many different institutions. Significant work is being done by the various charitable agencies: *Misereor, Adveniat, Missio, Renovabis,* as well as diocesan and parish *Caritas* organizations. Equally vast is the educational work carried out in Catholic schools and other Catholic institutions and organizations on behalf of young people. These are just a few brief examples, incomplete yet significant, which sketch as it were the portrait of a living Church, the Church which gave birth to us in faith and which we have the honor and the joy to serve.

MEETING WITH THE GERMAN BISHOPS,
AUGUST 21, 2005

FAMILY AND YOUTH: THE "DOMESTIC CHURCH"

Forming Authentic Christian Families

*T*he family [is] besieged in our days by serious challenges represented by the different ideologies and by customs that undermine the very foundation of marriage and of the Christian family. Attention must then be given to family catechesis and to a positive and correct vision of matrimony and of conjugal morality, thus contributing to the formation of authentic Christian families that are distinguished by their visible experience of Gospel values. A Christian family, a true "domestic church," will also be a seedbed for abundant and holy vocations.

LETTER TO THE PRESIDENT OF THE LATIN AMERICAN
EPISCOPAL COUNCIL, MAY 14, 2005

Foundation of the Family

I myself had the opportunity to be the General Relator at the Special Assembly of the Synod of Bishops on the Family, celebrated in Rome in 1980 [The *Relator* is appointed by the pope, and, as the key leader, his job is to facilitate discussion and foster consensus on the synod's conclusions]. The Apostolic Exhortation

Familiaris Consortio that resulted from this
Assembly makes a deep analysis of the identity
and mission of the family, which it describes as
the "domestic Church" and sanctuary of life.

Today, if they are to give a truly human face
to society, no people can ignore the precious
good of the family, founded on marriage. "The
matrimonial covenant, by which a man and a
woman establish between themselves a
partnership of the whole of life, is by its nature
ordered toward the good of the spouses and the
procreation and education of offspring" (can.
1055): this is the foundation of the family and
the patrimony and common good of humanity.

Thus, the Church cannot cease to proclaim
that in accordance with God's plans (see
Matthew 19:3–9), marriage and the family are
irreplaceable and permit no other alternatives.

Today more than ever, the Christian family
has a very noble mission that it cannot shirk: the
transmission of the faith, which involves the gift
of self to Jesus Christ who died and rose, and
insertion into the Ecclesial Community.

Parents are the first evangelizers of children,
a precious gift from the Creator (see *Gaudium
et Spes*, n. 50), and begin by teaching them to
say their first prayers. In this way a moral
universe is built up, rooted in the will of God,

where the child grows in the human and
Christian values that give life its full meaning.

LETTER TO THE PARTICIPANTS OF THE FIFTH WORLD
MEETING OF FAMILIES, MAY 17, 2005

Fully Open to Christ

If we look at these young people who were
gathered around the late pope, and as a result,
around Christ, whose cause the pope espoused,
something just as comforting could be seen: it is
not true that young people think only of
consumerism and pleasure. It is not true that
they are materialistic and self-centered. Just the
opposite is true: young people want great
things. They want an end to injustice. They
want inequalities to be overcome and all
peoples to have their share in the earth's goods.
They want freedom for the oppressed. They
want great things, good things.

This is why young people are—you are—
once again fully open to Christ. Christ did not
promise an easy life. Those who desire comforts
have dialed the wrong number. Rather, he
shows us the way to great things, the good,
towards an authentic human life.

ADDRESS TO GERMAN PILGRIMS IN ROME,
APRIL 25, 2005

Hope for the Church

Precisely with regard to the young, their formation and their relationship with the Lord and with the Church, I would like to add a final word. In fact, as John Paul II often repeated, they are the hope of the Church; but in today's world, they are also particularly vulnerable to the risk of being "tossed here and there, carried about by every wind of doctrine" (Ephesians 4:14).

Hence, they must be helped to grow and develop in the faith: this is the first service they should receive from the Church and especially from us bishops and our priests. We know well that many of them cannot understand and accept all the Church's teaching straightaway, but for this very reason it is important to reawaken within them the desire to believe with the Church, to trust that this Church, enlivened and guided by the Spirit, is the true subject of faith and that by becoming part of her we enter and participate in the communion of faith.

If this is to happen, young people must feel loved by the Church and concretely loved by us bishops and priests. In this way they will experience in the Church the Lord's friendship and love for them and understand that in Christ, truth coincides with love. In turn, they will learn to love the Lord and to trust in his Body, which is the Church.

ADDRESS TO ITALIAN BISHOPS CONFERENCE, MAY 30, 2005

The Holy Family

Sustained by the paternal care of Joseph, Mary welcomed her Son. In the home of Nazareth, Jesus reached adulthood, in the bosom of a family, humanly splendid and pervaded by the divine mystery. It continues to be a model for all families.

In this regard, the family, through home life, fulfills its human and Christian vocation, sharing joys and hopes in an atmosphere of understanding and reciprocal help. Therefore, the human being who is born, develops and is formed in the family, is able to start out on the journey of good without hesitation, without allowing himself or herself to be disoriented by customs or ideologies unworthy of the human person.

LETTER ON THE OCCASION OF THE NATIONAL PILGRIMAGE TO THE SHRINE OF NUESTRA SEÑORA DEL PILAR OF SARAGOSSA, MAY 19, 2005

A Sign of God's Faithful Love

The family is called to be an "intimate partnership of life and love" (Pastoral Constitution *Gaudium et Spes*, n. 48), because it is founded on indissoluble marriage. Despite the difficulties and the social and cultural conditioning of this period of history, Christian spouses must not cease to be in their lives a sign of God's faithful love: may they collaborate actively with priests in the pastoral guidance of engaged couples, young married couples and families, and in bringing up the new generations.

ADDRESS TO PILGRIMS FROM THE
DIOCESE OF VERONA, JUNE 4, 2005

Formed in the Image of God

For two years now the missionary commitment of the Church of Rome has focused above all on the family. This is not only because today this fundamental human reality is subjected to a multitude of problems and threats and is therefore especially in need of evangelization and practical support, but also because Christian families constitute a crucial resource for education in the faith, for the edification of the Church as communion and for her ability to be a missionary presence in the most varied situations of life, as well as to act as a Christian leaven in the widespread culture and social structures….

The assumption from which it is necessary to set out, if we are to understand the family mission in the Christian community and its tasks of forming the person and transmitting the faith, is always that of the meaning of marriage and the family in the plan of God, Creator and Savior….

Marriage and the family are not in fact a chance sociological construction, the product of particular historical and financial situations. On the other hand, the question of the right relationship between the man and the woman is rooted in the essential core of the human being and it is only by starting from here that its response can be found.

…[I]t cannot be separated from the ancient but ever new human question: Who am I? What is a human being? And this question, in turn, cannot be separated from the question about God: Does God exist? Who is God? What is his face truly like?

The Bible gives one consequential answer to

these two queries: the human being is created in the image of God, and God himself is love. It is therefore the vocation to love that makes the human person an authentic image of God: man and woman come to resemble God to the extent that they become loving people.

…God could take the history of love and of the union of a man and a woman in the covenant of marriage as a symbol of salvation history. The inexpressible fact, the mystery of God's love for men and women, receives its linguistic form from the vocabulary of marriage and the family, both positive and negative: indeed, God's drawing close to his people is presented in the language of spousal love, whereas Israel's infidelity, its idolatry, is designated as adultery and prostitution.

In the New Testament God radicalizes his love to the point that he himself becomes, in his Son, flesh of our flesh, a true man. In this way, God's union with humankind acquired its supreme, irreversible form.

…The sacramental quality that marriage assumes in Christ, therefore, means that the gift of creation has been raised to the grace of redemption. Christ's grace is not an external addition to human nature, it does not do violence to men and women but sets them free and restores them, precisely by raising them above their own limitations. And just as the Incarnation of the Son of God reveals its true meaning in the cross, so genuine human love is self-giving and cannot exist if it seeks to detach itself from the Cross.

...[I]n the begetting of children marriage reflects its divine model, God's love for man. In man and woman, fatherhood and motherhood, like the body and like love, cannot be limited to the biological: life is entirely given only when, by birth, love and meaning are also given, which make it possible to say yes to this life.

From this point it becomes clear how contrary to human love, to the profound vocation of the man and the woman, are the systematic closure of a union to the gift of life and even more, the suppression or manipulation of newborn life.

No man and no woman, however, alone and single-handed, can adequately transmit to children love and the meaning of life. Indeed, to be able to say to someone "your life is good, even though I may not know your future," requires an authority and credibility superior to what individuals can assume on their own.

Christians know that this authority is

conferred upon that larger family which God, through his Son Jesus Christ and the gift of the Holy Spirit, created in the story of humanity, that is, upon the Church. Here they recognize the work of that eternal, indestructible love which guarantees permanent meaning to the life of each one of us, even if the future remains unknown.

For this reason, the edification of each individual Christian family fits into the context of the larger family of the Church, which supports it and carries it with her and guarantees that it has, and will also have in the future, the meaningful "yes" of the Creator. And the Church is reciprocally built up by the family, a "small domestic church," as the Second Vatican Council called it (*Lumen Gentium*, n. 11; *Apostolicam Actuositatem*, n. 11), rediscovering an ancient Patristic expression (see Saint John Chrysostom, *In Genesim Serm.* VI, 2; VII, 1).

In the same sense, *Familiaris Consortio* affirms that "Christian marriage...constitutes the natural setting in which the human person is introduced into the great family of the Church" (n. 15)....

Dear brothers and sisters, and especially you, dear priests, I am aware of the generosity and dedication with which you serve the Lord and the Church. Your daily work forming the new generations in the faith, in close connection with the sacraments of Christian initiation, as well as marriage preparation and offering guidance to families in their often difficult progress, particularly in the important task of raising children, is the fundamental way to regenerating the Church ever anew, and also to reviving the social fabric of our beloved city of Rome.

Continue, therefore, without letting yourselves be discouraged by the difficulties you encounter. The educational relationship is delicate by nature: in fact, it calls into question the freedom of the other who, however gently, is always led to make a decision. Neither parents nor priests nor catechists, nor any other educators can substitute for the freedom of the child, adolescent or young person whom they are addressing. The proposal of Christianity in particular challenges the very essence of freedom and calls it to faith and conversion.

ADDRESS TO THE ECCLESIAL DIOCESAN CONVENTION OF ROME, JUNE 6, 2005

In Defense of the Family

The Church, accustomed as she is to scrutinizing God's will engraved in the very nature of the human creature, sees in the family a most important value that must be defended from any attack that aims to undermine its solidity and call its very existence into question.

ADDRESS TO THE PRESIDENT OF THE ITALIAN REPUBLIC, JUNE 24, 2005

$\mathcal{M}$ARY:
IN THE HANDS
OF OUR MOST
HOLY MOTHER

The Future of the Church

To support me in my promise, I call on the motherly intercession of Mary Most Holy, in whose hands I place the present and future of the Church and of myself.

FIRST MESSAGE TO THE MEMBERS OF THE COLLEGE OF CARDINALS, APRIL 20, 2005

Mother of the Church

I entrust all of us and the expectations, hopes and worries of the entire community of Christians to the Virgin Mother of God, who accompanied the steps of the newborn Church with her silent presence and comforted the faith of the apostles. I ask you to walk under the motherly protection of Mary, *Mater Ecclesiae* ["Mother of the Church"], docile and obedient to the voice of her divine Son, Our Lord Jesus Christ. As I call upon her constant patronage, I impart to each one of you and to all those whom divine Providence entrusts to your pastoral care my heartfelt Apostolic Blessing.

ADDRESS TO THE MEMBERS OF THE COLLEGE OF CARDINALS, APRIL 22, 2005

Mother of Our Lord

Let us walk together, let us be united. I trust in your help. I ask for your understanding if I make mistakes, as happens to any man, or if something that the pope has to say or do according to his own conscience or the conscience of the Church is not understood. I ask for your trust. If we stay united, then we will discover the right path. And let us pray to Mary, Mother of the Lord, so that she will enable us to feel her love as a woman and a mother, in which we can understand all of the depth of Christ's mystery.

ADDRESS TO GERMAN PILGRIMS, APRIL 25, 2005

With Mary's Eyes

I address my thoughts to Mary: the month of May is specially dedicated to her. Pope John Paul II taught us, with his words and even more, with his example, to contemplate Christ with Mary's eyes, especially appreciating the prayer of the Holy Rosary. With the singing of the *Regina Caeli*, let us entrust to the Blessed Virgin all the needs of the Church and of humanity.

REGINA CAELI, MAY 1, 2005

The Young, Sick, and Newlyweds

In this month of May dedicated especially to the Mother of the Lord, I invite you, dear young people, to learn from Mary to love and follow Christ above all things. May Our Lady help you, dear sick people, to look with faith at the mystery of pain and to grasp the saving value of every cross. I entrust you, dear newlyweds, to the motherly protection of the Blessed Virgin, so that you will live out in your own family the atmosphere of prayer and love of the home in Nazareth.

GENERAL AUDIENCE, MAY 4, 2005

Protection for the Church

After the Lord ascended to Heaven, the disciples gathered in prayer in the Upper Room, with the Mother of Jesus (see Acts 1:14), invoking together the Holy Spirit who would invest them with the power to witness to the Risen Christ (see Luke 24:49; Acts 1:8). United to the Most Blessed Virgin, every Christian community relives in these days this unique spiritual experience in preparation for

the solemnity of Pentecost. We too turn now to
Mary with the hymn of the *Regina Caeli*,
imploring her protection on the Church and
especially on those who dedicate themselves to
the work of evangelization through the means
of social communication.

REGINA CAELI, WORLD COMMUNICATIONS DAY,
MAY 8, 2005

Our Lady of Guadalupe

Holy Mary, who under the title of Our
Lady of Guadalupe are invoked as Mother by
the men and women of Mexico and of Latin
America, encouraged by the love that you
inspire in us, we once again place our life in
your motherly hands.

May you, who are present in these Vatican
Gardens, hold sway in the hearts of all the
mothers of the world.

Our Lady of Guadalupe, pray for us.

PRAYER BEFORE THE IMAGE OF OUR LADY
OF GUADALUPE, MAY 11, 2005

A Renewed Outpouring
of the Spirit

We entrust this hope to the intercession of the Virgin Mary, who today we contemplate in the glorious mystery of Pentecost. The Holy Spirit, who at Nazareth descended upon her to make her the Mother of the Word Incarnate (see Luke 1:35), descended today on the nascent Church joined together around her in the Upper Room (see Acts 1:14). We invoke with trust Mary Most Holy, in order to obtain a renewed outpouring of the Spirit on the Church in our days.

REGINA CAELI, PENTECOST, MAY 15, 2005

Caring for Every Human Life

I place all your worries and aspirations at the feet of the Virgin, trusting in the fact that the Holy Spirit will move many people so that they generously love life and welcome the poor, loving them with God's same love.

To Mary Most Holy, who generated the Author of life, I entrust every human life from the first moment of its existence until its natural death. I ask her to protect all families from every kind of social injustice, from all that degrades their dignity and threatens their freedom; and for respect for religious freedom and the freedom of conscience of every person.

[I] encourage each and all to live in your particular Church in a spirit of communion and of service, and I exhort you to give devout witness to the Virgin Mary and to tireless love of neighbor.

LETTER ON THE OCCASION OF THE NATIONAL PILGRIMAGE TO THE SHRINE OF NUESTRA SEÑORA DEL PILAR OF SARAGOSSA, MAY 19, 2005

Woman of the Eucharist

Our Lady accompanies us every day in our prayers. During this special Year of the Eucharist in which we are living, Mary helps us above all to discover ever better the great sacrament of the Eucharist.

In his last Encyclical, *Ecclesia de Eucharistia*, our beloved Pope John Paul II presented her to us as "Woman of the Eucharist" throughout her life (see number 53). "Woman of the Eucharist" through and through, beginning with her inner disposition: from the Annunciation, when she offered herself for the Incarnation of the Word of God, to the Cross and to the Resurrection;

"Woman of the Eucharist" in the period subsequent to Pentecost, when she received in the Sacrament that Body which she had conceived and carried in her womb.

…[W]e pause to meditate on the mystery of the Visitation of the Virgin to Saint Elizabeth. Mary went to see her elderly cousin Elizabeth, whom everyone said was sterile but who instead had reached the sixth month of a pregnancy given to her by God (see Luke 1:36), carrying in her womb the recently conceived Jesus. She was a young girl but she was not afraid, for God was with her, within her.

In a certain way we can say that her journey was…the first "Eucharistic procession" in history. Mary, living Tabernacle of God made flesh, is the Ark of the Covenant in whom the Lord visited and redeemed his people. Jesus' presence filled her with the Holy Spirit.

When she entered Elizabeth's house, her greeting was overflowing with grace: John leapt in his mother's womb, as if he were aware of the coming of the One whom he would one day proclaim to Israel. The children exulted, the mothers exulted. This meeting, imbued with the joy of the Holy Spirit, is expressed in the Canticle of the Magnificat.

Is this not also the joy of the Church, which

ceaselessly welcomes Christ in the holy Eucharist and brings him into the world with the testimony of active charity, steeped in faith and hope? Yes, welcoming Jesus and bringing him to others is the true joy of Christians!

Dear Brothers and Sisters, let us follow and imitate Mary, a deeply Eucharistic soul, and our whole life can become a Magnificat (see *Ecclesia de Eucharistia*, number 58), praise of God. May this be the grace that we ask from the Virgin Most Holy…My Blessing to you all.

ADDRESS AT THE CONCLUSION
OF THE MARIAN MONTH OF MAY, MAY 31, 2005

Heart of Christ, Heart of Mary

The heart that resembles that of Christ more than any other is without a doubt the Heart of Mary, his Immaculate Mother, and for this very reason the liturgy holds them up together for our veneration. Responding to the Virgin's invitation at Fátima, let us entrust the whole world to her Immaculate Heart, which we contemplated yesterday in a special way, so that it may experience the merciful love of God and know true peace.

ANGELUS, JUNE 5, 2005

The Perfect Model of Holiness

Mary Most Holy is a sublime and perfect model of holiness who lived in constant and profound communion with Christ. Let us invoke her intercession, together with the intercession of Saint Benedict, so that in our time too the Lord will multiply men and women who, through witnessing to an enlightened faith in their lives, may be the salt of the earth and the light of the world in this new millennium.

ANGELUS, JULY 10, 2005

$\mathcal{E}$PILOGUE

All of us belong to the communion of saints,
we who have been baptized in the name of the
Father, and of the Son, and of the Holy Spirit,
we who draw life from the gift of Christ's Body
and Blood, through which he transforms us and
makes us like himself.

Yes, the Church is alive....And the Church
is young. She holds within herself the future of
the world and therefore shows each of us the
way towards the future. The Church is alive
and we are seeing it: we are experiencing the
joy that the Risen Lord promised his followers.
The Church is alive—she is alive because
Christ is alive, because He is truly risen.

HOMILY FOR IMPOSITION OF THE PALLIUM AND
CONFERRAL OF THE FISHERMAN'S RING, APRIL 24, 2005